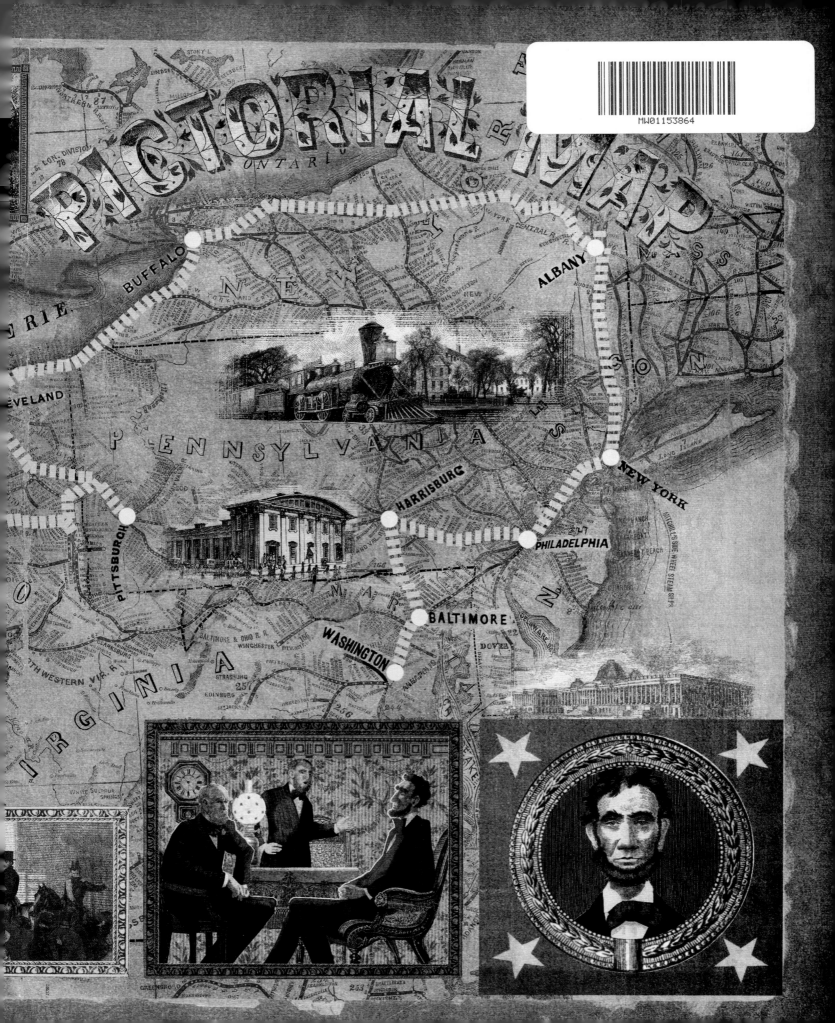

HIDING
in Plain Sight

PINKERTON
NATIONAL
DETECTIVE
AGENCY

Kate Warne and the Race to Save Abraham Lincoln

Written by
Beth Anderson

Illustrated by
Sally Wern Comport

CALKINS CREEK
AN IMPRINT OF ASTRA BOOKS FOR YOUNG READERS, *New York*

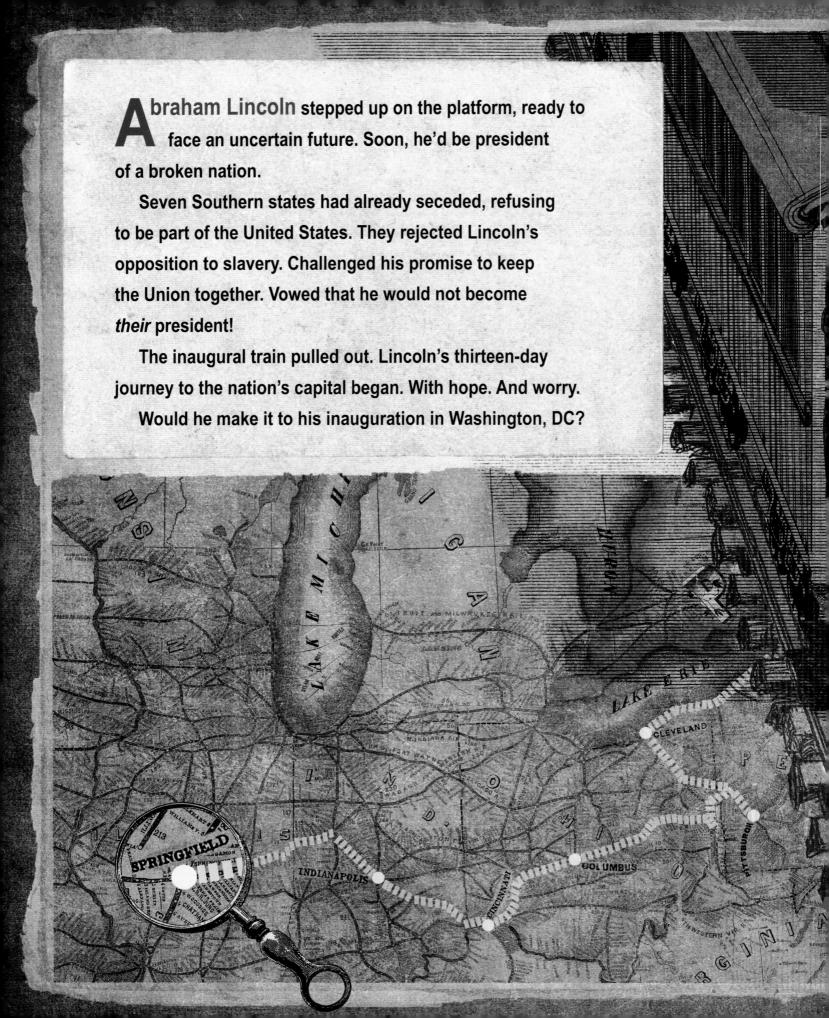

Abraham Lincoln stepped up on the platform, ready to face an uncertain future. Soon, he'd be president of a broken nation.

Seven Southern states had already seceded, refusing to be part of the United States. They rejected Lincoln's opposition to slavery. Challenged his promise to keep the Union together. Vowed that he would not become *their* president!

The inaugural train pulled out. Lincoln's thirteen-day journey to the nation's capital began. With hope. And worry.

Would he make it to his inauguration in Washington, DC?

"Mrs. Barley" wasn't who she appeared to be. But with her Alabama accent and outrage against Lincoln, she fit right in.

Saturday at noon, the president-elect would visit Baltimore on his way to the capital—his only pass into Southern territory. He wasn't welcome. And the city sizzled with anger. How far would people go to stop him?

Mrs. Barley eavesdropped on rebel talk.

Coaxed out secrets.

Scanned the hotel parlor.

In the doorway, she caught a signal.

And slipped upstairs to her room.

5

Tap . . . tap . . . tap . . .

Kate Warne opened the door, and Allan Pinkerton ducked inside.

Before she could report what she'd just uncovered, her boss's face confirmed the worst.

The plot to kill Lincoln in Baltimore was real!

The detectives had to act—find a way to foil the plot!

They couldn't change Lincoln's route. The only way to Washington was through Baltimore.

They *could* change the time . . . and the train . . .

But first they had to convince Mr. Lincoln his life was in danger.

With spies lurking about, Pinkerton didn't trust the telegraph. But he trusted Kate.

She must deliver a message.

To Mr. Judd, Lincoln's assistant.

Tomorrow.

Kate rushed to catch the train for New York City.

They had five days to save Lincoln.

NEW YORK

PHILADELPHIA

HARRISBURG

BALTIMORE

WASHINGTON

9

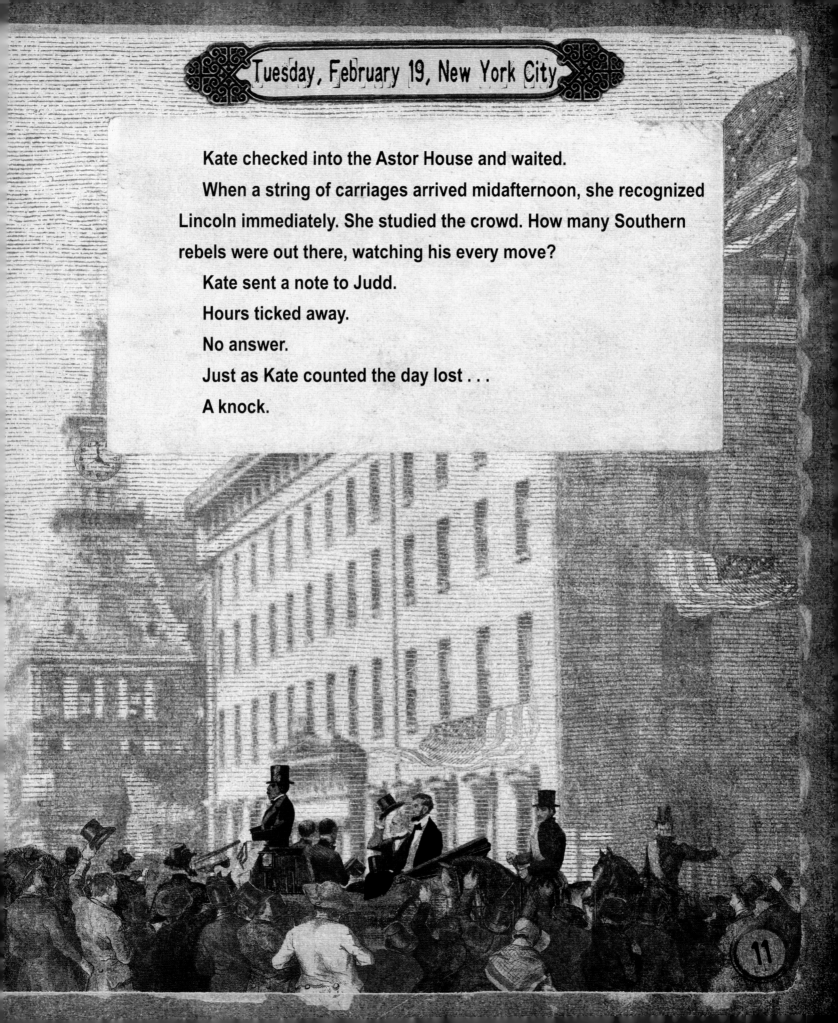

Kate checked into the Astor House and waited.

When a string of carriages arrived midafternoon, she recognized Lincoln immediately. She studied the crowd. How many Southern rebels were out there, watching his every move?

Kate sent a note to Judd.

Hours ticked away.

No answer.

Just as Kate counted the day lost . . .

A knock.

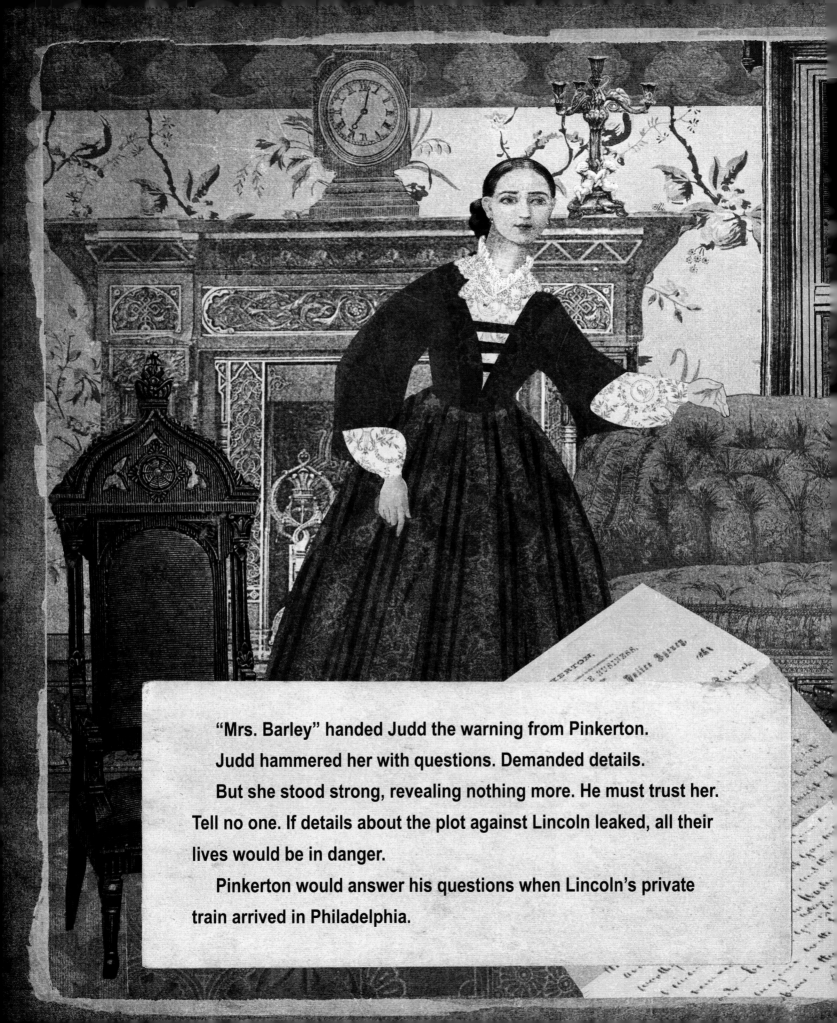

"Mrs. Barley" handed Judd the warning from Pinkerton.

Judd hammered her with questions. Demanded details.

But she stood strong, revealing nothing more. He must trust her. Tell no one. If details about the plot against Lincoln leaked, all their lives would be in danger.

Pinkerton would answer his questions when Lincoln's private train arrived in Philadelphia.

Could Pinkerton convince Lincoln to skip tomorrow's events?

Convince him to sneak through Baltimore ahead of schedule?

Convince him that he *must leave tonight*?

When the night train's whistle wailed with no word from her boss, Kate knew . . .

Their plan had failed.

Lincoln had refused to cancel events.
But, he agreed to trust the detectives to get him through
Baltimore—*after* his afternoon visit to Harrisburg.

Kate and Pinkerton had one more chance.

One more night train.

And now, one more complication. They had to get Lincoln back to Philadelphia to catch the night train—in just twenty hours.

Kate and Pinkerton double-checked details.

Still, there were plenty of opportunities for error.

What if someone saw Lincoln board the special train in Harrisburg?

What if they tried to send a message?

And most troublesome—

What if Lincoln didn't arrive in Philadelphia in time?

They needed a ruse, a reason to make the night train wait.

A package!

Pinkerton made arrangements.

The conductor was ordered to wait for an important package!

Every piece was in place. Now, Kate had to trust . . . and hope Southern spies didn't spot something suspicious.

In a few hours, Lincoln's life would be in her hands.

Finally, the mission was underway. Railroad executives cleared the route. Telegraph officials disabled the lines. The train raced to Philadelphia at top speed.

Kate breathed deep, pushing back her nerves. Was she ready for the greatest challenge of her life?

While Pinkerton waited for Lincoln to arrive at another station across town, Kate took on a new identity.

In the depot, "Mrs. Cherry" bought tickets—including one for her "sick brother."

She boarded, and chose four berths. In the rear. Away from curious eyes.

But other passengers wanted those berths.

She pleaded with the conductor and slipped him a silver coin. Her frail brother needed quiet.

While the conductor kept others away, she peered into the darkness . . .

Three men emerged from the shadows.

Mrs. Cherry greeted "her brother" and snugged the shawl over his beard.

She ushered him to a berth. And drew the curtain.

A man handed the conductor the package he'd been waiting for.

The whistle pierced the air.

Mrs. Cherry kept watch as the train pushed south for Baltimore. If word had leaked that the president-elect was on the train, an attack would be easy.

Lincoln's quiet joking eased her heart, but not the danger.

The train pulled into the station as Baltimore slept.
Mrs. Cherry checked the platform, then said
goodbye to "her brother."

RAIL ROAD CAR TRANSFER ROUTE THROUGH BALTIMORE

CAMDEN ST. STATION

PRESIDENT ST. STATION

EUTAW ST.
HOWARD ST.
SHARP ST.
HANOVER ST.
CHARLES ST.
LIGHT ST.
CALVERT ST.
SOUTH ST.
COMMERCE ST.
GAY ST.
FREDERICK ST.
CENTRE MARKET
HARFORD ST.
PRESIDENT ST.

PRATT

EAST PRATT ST.

CAMDEN ST.

CONWAY ST.

BARRE ST.

LEE ST.

LIGHT ST. WHARF

BASIN

CITY SPRING DOCK

LONG DOCK

CANTON

ALICE ANNA ST.

EASTERN AVE.

TRINITY ST.

LANCASTER ST.

CITY DOCK

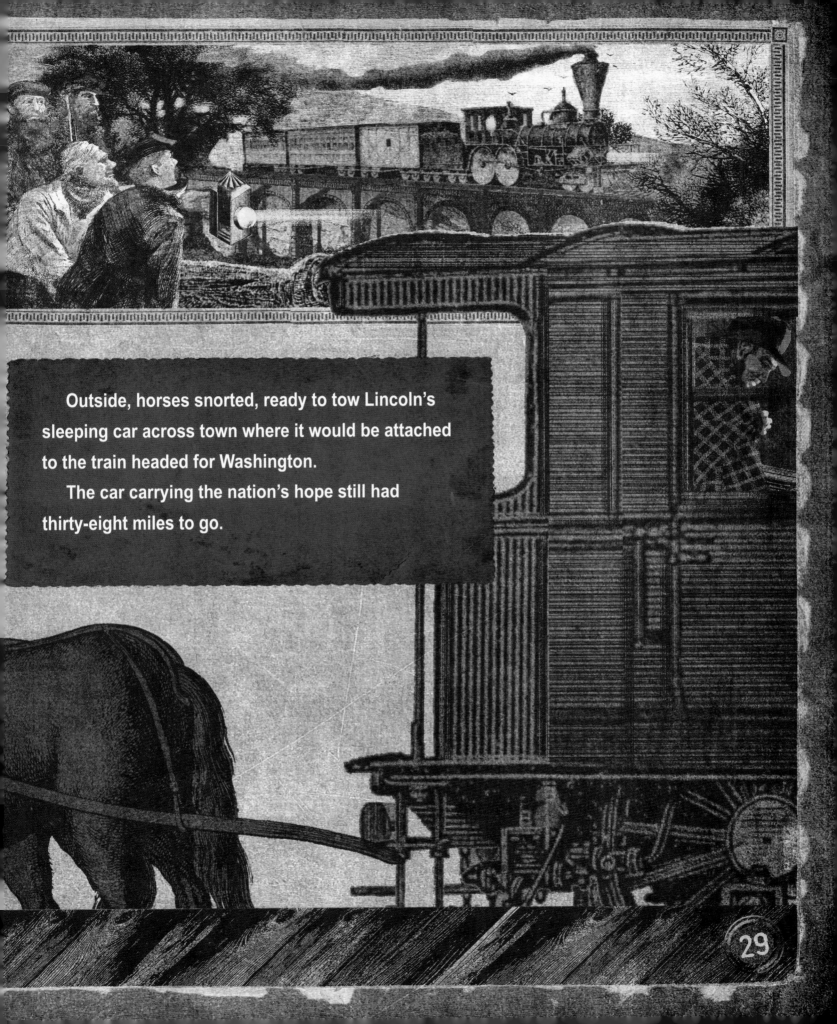

Outside, horses snorted, ready to tow Lincoln's sleeping car across town where it would be attached to the train headed for Washington.

The car carrying the nation's hope still had thirty-eight miles to go.

Hours later, "Mrs. Barley" joined the crowds awaiting the arrival of the inaugural train.

First came the rumors.

Then the news reports.

Lincoln was already in Washington!

Mrs. Barley gasped, joining the Southern outrage.

But in her heart, the detective celebrated. Lincoln was safe!

Kate Warne melted into the crowd, eyes and ears on alert for more threats to the president and the nation.

She would remain undercover.

Hiding in plain sight.

Ever ready for her next assignment.

AFTERWORD

Though many called Abraham Lincoln a coward for sneaking through Baltimore, the nation would soon recognize the tall, bearded man with the stovepipe hat for the strong leader he was.

Pinkerton kept quiet about the role the detectives played until others questioned the truth of the plot. In 1868, he revealed that a railroad official had hired the investigators after being warned about sabotage by Southern rebels and dangers to Lincoln. Pinkerton's account included testimony from Judd, the railroad official, the man who unlocked the back door of the sleeping car, and the man who cut the telegraph wires in Harrisburg.

Unknown to Pinkerton at the time of the incident, government agents were also investigating threats against Lincoln in Baltimore. Hours after speaking with Pinkerton in Philadelphia, Lincoln received a note from his soon-to-be secretary of state, William Seward. It, too, warned of an assassination plot in Baltimore and urged the president-elect to change his schedule. This second warning likely contributed to Lincoln's decision to accept Pinkerton's plan.

The painting *Farewell to Illinois* by Reynolds Jones shows Lincoln leaving Springfield, IL, for Washington, DC, February 11, 1861.

Kate Warne

America's First Female Detective

Kate Warne, a young widow, became the first female detective in the United States when Allan Pinkerton hired her in 1856. Demonstrating her power of persuasion, she convinced him that women could gain access to people and places that men could not. She quickly proved herself as a trusted employee and excellent detective, and soon became the supervisor of Pinkerton's Female Detective Bureau. Following her work in Baltimore, she went on to support Lincoln by spying for the Union in the Civil War. Kate died of an unknown illness in 1868.

Kate Warne has left us with many questions. There is little information about her life before she walked into Pinkerton's office. And unfortunately, many of the agency's records of this time were lost in a fire. Kate Warne remains one of history's fascinating mysteries.

The Pinkerton National Detective Agency logo: "The Eye that Never Sleeps"

Abraham Lincoln and Slavery

The history of Abraham Lincoln's views on slavery is complicated. But in order to understand why Southerners were so violently against him, it helps to know his views at the time of his inaugural journey.

Lincoln had stated his opposition to slavery when he ran for president in 1860. He vowed not to let it spread to new states as they were added to the country, thinking that would help the institution end soon on its own. The president had no power to abolish slavery, yet Southern slave owners and society saw him as a threat to their way of life. Very few Southerners voted for him, and they rejected him as their president.

A Note on the Railroads

At the time of Lincoln's journey to Washington, different railroad companies owned different routes. Many tracks weren't connected through cities, and each line went into a different depot. Because of this, passengers traveling through a city often had to go across town to another depot to catch the next leg of their trip. In Philadelphia, Lincoln had to take a carriage from one station to another. In Baltimore, horses pulled his sleeping car through the streets and attached it to another train for the final leg of the trip. This transfer created an additional danger by exposing him to the public.

Disguise and Deception

Sometimes the best protection is deception. And the best deception often takes advantage of appearances and assumptions about people.

GREAT WESTERN RAILROAD.

TIME CARD

For a Special Train, Monday, Feb. 11, 1861,

WITH

His Excellency, Abraham Lincoln, President Elect.

Leave	SPRINGFIELD,	8.00	A. M.
"	JAMESTOWN,	8.15	"
"	DAWSON,	8.24	"
"	MECHANICSBURG,	8.30	"
"	LANESVILLE,	8.37	"
"	ILLIOPOLIS	8.49	"
"	NIANTIC.	8.58	"
"	SUMMIT,	9.07	'
Arrive at	DECATUR,	9.24	"
Leave	DECATUR.	9.29	"
"	OAKLEY,	9.45	"
"	CERRO GORDO,	9.54	"
"	BEMENT,	10.13	"
"	SADORUS,	19.40	"
Arrive at	TOLONO,	10.50	"
Leave	"	10.55	"
"	PHILO,	11.07	"
"	SIDNEY,	11.17	"
"	HOMER,	11.30	"
"	SALINA,	11.45	"
"	CATLIN,	11.59	"
"	BRYANT,	12.07	P. M.
"	DANVILLE,	12.12	"
Arrive at	STATE LINE,	12.30	P. M.

This train will be entitled to the road, *and all other trains must be kept out of the way.*

Trains to be passed and met must be on the side track at least 10 minutes before this train is due.

Agents at all stations between Springfield and State Line must be on duty when this train passes, and examine the switches and know *that all is right before it passes.*

Operators at Telegraph Stations between Springfield and State Line must remain on duty until this train passes, and immediately report its time to Chas. H. Speed, Springfield.

All Foremen and men under their direction must be on the track and know positively that the track is in order.

It is very important that this train should pass over the road in safety, and all employees are expected to render all assistance in their power.

Red is the signal for danger, but any signal apparently intended to indicate alarm or danger must be regarded, the train stopped, and the meaning of it ascertained.

Carefulness is particularly enjoined.

F. W. BOWEN,
Supt.

This time card shows the stops on the first day of Lincoln's inaugural train journey.

Looking the Part

Pinkerton needed to be able to infiltrate all levels of society—including the upper class which provided money for the plot. Kate Warne's role as a "southern belle" was essential. In Baltimore, she dressed as a high-society woman with hoop skirts and fancy clothes. The black-and-white cockade pinned to her dress was a finishing touch. It marked her as a supporter of secession and the Southern cause, just like people today might wear ribbons or pins to show their support for a cause. Speaking with a southern accent, she sounded like one of them, too. But when she delivered the message to Lincoln's assistant in New York City, she dressed and acted differently. She was all business so that Judd would take her seriously. Whatever Kate's role, she used clothing to present the image needed for her assignments.

This image is generally accepted as a portrait of Kate Warne from 1866, but historians are unable to verify if it is actually her.

Well-Chosen Words

Kate was a skilled conversationalist who earned the trust of others. She knew when to talk and when to listen. She chose her words well, and by using flattery and empathy, encouraged others to let down their guard and reveal secrets. In New York City, she used stern words of warning with Judd because most men at the time were unlikely to take advice from women. When she spoke to the train conductor about holding the berths, she appealed to him emotionally, so he'd be more willing to help.

Advantage in Assumptions

People tend to trust their eyes and judge others by their appearance. Because of this, both Abraham Lincoln and Kate Warne were underestimated.

Thousands came out to see Lincoln on his way to Washington, DC. While some saw a compassionate man who inspired their faith, many were disappointed. He didn't look handsome or heroic; he didn't look like a president. Unusually tall and gangly, and without formal schooling, he was seen by many as unsophisticated, uneducated, and unsuited to be president—especially with the nation in crisis.

In Kate's time, women were considered weak and dependent. She used that to her advantage. Few would suspect the reality—that she was incredibly smart, courageous, and working undercover. Although most of us know that looks can be deceiving, we can easily get caught in that trap.

As a widow, Kate was independent and not tied to a traditional female role. Typically, when a woman's husband died, she had to take on his responsibilities and find a way to make a living. This situation gave Kate the opportunity to choose an unusual career—one that made the most of her acting talents, quick mind, and attention to detail, as well as her sense of adventure. It would be more than forty years before police departments hired female investigators. Not only did Kate Warne impact history with her role in protecting Lincoln, but she also opened up careers in investigation for women.

Need-to-Know

As most of us know, it's hard to keep a secret. The Pinkerton detectives told those assisting them only the details needed to do their part—nothing extra. This is called a need-to-know basis. Kate refused to reveal additional information to Judd because if those details became known to Southern rebels, it would have been easy for them to figure out who the undercover agents were. A need-to-know basis helps keep people safe and a plan secure.

Abraham Lincoln safely arrives in Washington, DC, after secretly passing through Baltimore, February 23, 1861.

Code Names

The detectives used aliases and code names in messages. (And it appears Allan Pinkerton liked names of foods.) In this incident, Kate used several aliases—Mrs. Barley and Mrs. Cherry. One of Pinkerton's aliases, E. J. Allen, can be found in the telegraph message he sent to Lincoln's party in Philadelphia to let them know the president-elect had arrived safely in Washington, DC:

"Plums arrived here with Nuts this morning—all right. —E. J. Allen."

It's a strange-sounding message, using "Plums" for Pinkerton and "Nuts" for Lincoln!

By using code names and not revealing their accomplishments, the detectives protected their identities and were able to continue their work. If the newspapers had shared the story of how Kate and Pinkerton sneaked Lincoln through Baltimore, everyone would have been watching them. Protecting their identities also meant they gave up any glory they might have received.

Many hidden heroes of history go unrecognized through the ages—people who did what was needed to protect the greater good. In the case of the Baltimore Plot, the detectives worked to preserve the power of the people in a democracy, ensuring that the candidate voters had elected became president.

Allan Pinkerton (left) and Abraham Lincoln (center) at Antietam, MD, 1862

BIBLIOGRAPHY

All quotations used in the book can be found in the following sources marked with an asterisk (*).

PRIMARY SOURCE

Pinkerton, Allan. *The Spy of the Rebellion: Being a True History of the Spy System of the United States Army During the Late Rebellion. Revealing Many Secrets of the War Hitherto Not Made Public. Compiled from Official Reports Prepared for President Lincoln, General McClellan and the Provost-Marshal-General.* Hartford: M. A. Winter & Hatch, 1883.

EDITED COLLECTIONS OF PRIMARY SOURCE MATERIAL

*Cuthbert, Norma Briggs, ed. *Lincoln and the Baltimore Plot 1861 from Pinkerton Records and Related Papers.* San Marino, CA: Huntington Library, 1949.

Library of Congress. *With Malice Toward None: The Abraham Lincoln Bicentennial Exhibition, The Journey of the President-Elect.* 2009, interactive presentation. loc.gov/exhibits/lincoln/interactives/journey-of-the-president-elect.

Miers, Earl Schenck, and C. Percy Powell, eds. *Lincoln Day by Day: A Chronology 1809–1865* vol. III: 1861–1865. Washington: Lincoln Sesquicentennial Commission, 1960.

SECONDARY SOURCES

Arnold, Isaac N. "The Baltimore Plot to Assassinate Abraham Lincoln," *Harper's New Monthly Magazine* 37, no. 217 (June 1868): 123–28.

Kline, Michael J. *The Baltimore Plot: The First Conspiracy to Assassinate Abraham Lincoln.* Yardley, PA: Westholme Publishing, 2008.

Meltzer, Brad and Josh Mensch. *The Lincoln Conspiracy: The Secret Plot to Kill America's 16th President—and Why It Failed.* New York: Flatiron Books, 2020.

Ramsland, Katherine. "KATE WARNE: First Female Detective." *Forensic Examiner* 19, no. 1 (Spring 2010): 70–72.

Stashower, Daniel. *The Hour of Peril: The Secret Plot to Murder Lincoln Before the Civil War.* New York: Minotaur Books, 2013.

———. "The Unsuccessful Plot to Kill Abraham Lincoln." *Smithsonian* magazine, Feb. 2013.

Trostel, Scott D. *The Lincoln Inaugural Train: The 1861 Journey of President-elect Abraham Lincoln to Washington, D.C.* Fletcher, OH: Cam-Tech Publishing, 2011.

*Widmer, Ted. *Lincoln on the Verge: Thirteen Days to Washington.* New York: Simon & Schuster, 2020.

Wolly, Brian. "Lincoln's Whistle-Stop Trip to Washington." *Smithsonian* magazine, Feb. 9, 2011.

ILLUSTRATOR'S NOTE

The illustrations in this book were inspired by the Winterthur Museum, Garden, and Library and their collage albums (also known as scrapbook houses) in their Digital Collections. This sampling of the popular art form and other notable collections dating from the 1850s through the 1900s, informed the unusual decorative details and surreal perspectives that were a delight to discover, create anew, and transform into these page scenes. To explore the Winterthur's collection of scrapbook houses, visit contentdm.winterthur.org/digital/collection/collage.

ACKNOWLEDGMENTS

With tremendous thanks to the many people who helped make this book come to life. First, my critique partners who cheered me on with valuable feedback—thank you Vivian, Julie, Lynn, Kristen, Maria, Heather, Michelle, Kate, and Stephie. Much appreciation to my agent, Stephanie Fretwell-Hill, and editor, Carolyn Yoder, for creating a path for my writing and making this journey of discovery possible. Gratitude goes to the many historians who preserve the past, with a special shout-out to the Library of Congress. Huge thanks to James M. Cornelius, PhD, secretary of the Abraham Lincoln Association, and author Daniel Stashower for their assistance ensuring historical accuracy. And to my family who inspires and encourages me in this endeavor—all my love.

To my sisters—by family and friendship—
always at the ready —*BA*

To my ever-faithful friend and workmate
Lindsay, who always with soul, matches
the task at hand. —*SWC*

PICTURE CREDITS

Library of Congress: gm70005368: endpapers, 2, 9, 16;
rc01003453: 28; scsm000375: 36; 2016850765: 38;
2018666254: 39. Courtesy of the Abraham Lincoln Presidential
Library & Museum: 34. Pinkerton Consulting & Investigations:
35. Chicago History Museum, ICHi-075012: 37.

For information about permission to reproduce
selections from this book, please contact
permissions@astrapublishinghouse.com.

Calkins Creek
An imprint of Astra Books for Young Readers,
a division of Astra Publishing House
astrapublishinghouse.com
Printed in China

ISBN: 978-1-63592-823-5 (hc)
ISBN: 978-1-63592-824-2 (eBook)
Library of Congress Control Number: 2024932217

First edition
10 9 8 7 6 5 4 3 2 1

Design by Barbara Grzeslo
The text is set in Arial Narrow.
The illustrations are created using drawings in pencil, traditional
collage, digital collage, and digital paint.

LAKE MICHIGAN

SPRINGFIELD

INDIANAPOLIS

CINCINNATI

COLUM

PINKERTON
NATIONAL
DETECTIVE